WOMEN IN MAYHEM
OR THREE NONSENSICAL PRANKS

By

DAVID WILLIAM PARRY

978-0-6486072-3-6

Women In Mayhem:
Or Three Nonsensical Pranks
David William Parry

©Manticore Press, Melbourne, Australia, 2024.

Cover Art: Arkle, William. *The Manna Within*. c.1950-59. Oil on canvas.

All rights reserved, no section of this book may be utilized without permission, except brief quotations, including electronic reproductions without the permission of the copyright holders and publisher. Published in Australia.

Thema Classification: DDC (Contemporary Plays), 5PS (LGBTQIA+).

INDIGO DRAGON
WWW.INDIGODRAGON.COM.AU

A gigantic thanky doodle to My Eternal Beloved DHI, global Anarchism, and the Martian poet Christopher Reid.

BY THE SAME AUTHOR

Caliban's Redemption
The Grammar of Witchcraft
Mount Athos Inside Me: Essays on Religion, Swedenborg and Arts

CONTENTS

Foundational Directions	7
PROLOGUE	9
PRANK 1 SURFACE TRUTHS	13
PRANK 2 A DAY IN THE LIGHT	25
PRANK 3 FATE'S GOOD FORTUNE	41
EPILOGUE	53
Notes	59
An Afterword By Reinhard Auer	61

FOUNDATIONAL DIRECTIONS

This three act conceptualist dramedy takes place in various Purgatories. Phrased differently, those psychic territories wherein souls are forced to wait for resolution. As such, our guide through these dreaded locations (the Dancing Pilot, or DP), introduces each character in turn before a specific tale unfolds, albeit in a manner suggesting they are actually the same people in different settings. Or, perhaps more suggestively, she implies such personae remain essentially the same although having a different ethnicity, gender and class in every scene. However, the DP might effectively be describing aspects of her own psyche, which is why she occasionally illustrates them in pen and ink on stage. Either way, two silver angels clear and set the performance area at the start of each enactment, while the audience is asked to give judgement on these character-concepts as an extension to the epilogue.

PROLOGUE

Stage directions.

A blackened performance space is energised through the song "Flying Down To Rio" as originally sung by Fred Astaire and interpreted by Ginger Rogers through her dancing. Images of King Kong fighting biplanes at the top of the Empire State Building are projected on to a blackened backdrop. When this tune is halfway through the houselights go up and the DP waltzes on to the stage dressed as a World War One pilot. She is quickly followed by two silver angels who place a flip chart stage right, alongside marker pens and voting cards.

(*Opening monologue.*)

DP

(*Looking at the audience.*)

Do I make you angry?
Either way, I have had enough of Rev. Parry
And his Marcelian psychodramas,

Quite enough of analogues and fantasy!
Likewise, my neighbours on chimney pots
Need fresh taboos and vacant promises
Beside debilitating Minions and Barbie dolls
Who thirst for far-off Chinatown.
Oh, Parry was a proud Hampshire ruffian
Still covered in clay
And a penniless bumpkin proving strong in th'arm
But not thick in th'head, because he could read and write
And drive a tractor (although never showing his legs luv,
Since he had legs to show), while his biggest flex
Was a predestination
Beyond Zero Hour Contracts and Continual Retraining
And Job Seekers Allowance and Rental Arrears
And Minimum Wages and a desperate Full Monty –
With a handshake on the way to an early scrapheap,
Since he had been invited to far-off Chinatown.

Beyond doubt it existed above British High Streets
And misplaced fanfares for a bygone suburbia
Beyond Primark, Superdrug, Greggs and Barclays

ANGELS

(*In officious unison.*)
I am sorry, but the queue starts here.

DP

Beyond a disunited Kingdom of colonial shadows
Cloaking racism, homophobia and class oppression
Beyond affluent agrarians and a posh nosh elite
Who never hungered for his far-off Chinatown,
Or the promise of oriental banqueting!

Yet, without age-old magic and green Jade rings
And dragons, red lanterns and Mandarin Jam
And Tai Chi classes, or late drinks in Ku Bar
Or gentle Tang poetry and Swallowtail butterflies
And silk napkins by Gong Fu cups of Oolong tea
Served in a pavilion behind three bamboo stalks
Aside pork dishes in sugar plus vinegar sauce
And Foo Dogs repelling every negative energy
Through bells and cymbals and drums and zithers
Alongside yellow banners near a Qing dynasty gate –
He would not prosper without Chinatown.

Now, lustreless conceits condemn average men
To darkening arts and merciless sins
Amid children bent double by limited hopes
In a medicinal Kingdom withholding its cures,
Which is why he eternally thirsted, ached,
Craved, hankered, and yearned,
For his glorious, far-off, Chinatown
And footslogged a step each and every inch

WOMEN IN MAYHEM

Towards a choreography of Calvino's thin city.

(*The angels leave stage left, whereas the DP stands immobile.*)

Lights Down.

PRANK ONE: SURFACE TRUTHS

Lights Up.

DP

Suffer the children of this prank. A middle aged cynic called Uncle, a destitute boy named Verne and a disembodied radio voice known to her followers as Zalmoxis.

ANGELS

(Offstage, chanting.)

Their monster tried to eat the Dancing Pilot. Their monster tried to eat the Dancing Pilot. Their monster tried to eat the Dancing Pilot. Their monster tried to eat the Dancing Pilot. Their monster tried to eat the Dancing Pilot.

(UNCLE enters stage left and stands brooding as well as barechested. He looks at a collection of books.

VERNE enters stage right wearing whipcord breeches, even though equally barechested. He rushes to wrestle with his uncle. They struggle for a few moments, before VERNE throws him onto the floor. As the VOICE sounds across the entire stage, images of Elijah Muhammad, Louis Farrakhan, Malcolm X, and depictions of the Hollow Earth, are projected on to the backdrop.)

VOICE

(*Echoes.*)

I am the Empress of Earth. Never noticed and always unseen, I am the hidden within. Yet, as the fiery force of every fantasy, I rule as the Empress of Earth.

VERNE

(*Listening to the voice, he confronts his UNCLE.*)

Incredible yarns, astonishing fables, and ripping tales. Unlike you, I have heard Her before. Her voice was the reason I travelled down craggy astral caverns, into ragged etheric caves, to see Her dark, chimerical, dwellings therein. Maybe, one day, I will write my adventures for everyone to read. Compelled, as it were, by the power of your parables, uncle. Through them, after all, I found my way to the legendary centre and experienced its searing heat. An internal Black Sun charbroiling, however . . .

(*Wipes forehead and chest with his hand.*)

an infernal atmosphere glorified through the overly intense and decadent rays of Her subterranean star. Since then, the memory of borrowing your meticulously written notebooks has burnt me!

(*Beat.*)

It's hot today. Too warm and unrepentantly overcast. Even though gloomily exhibiting definitional qualities. On such a delineated afternoon, I first read your occult diagrams and esoteric designs.

(*UNCLE groans.*)

Etchings, mysteriously charting – from ancient times – the landscape of an interior kingdom. A place of folklore, Lazeria maps, and mythology. Mere anecdotes, of course, even though they recount a realm beneath our dead. In areas, somehow, intertwined with the concept of failure: like the Christian Hell, the Greek underworld, the Jewish Sheol and more interestingly, the Nordic *Svartálfaheimr*. It was all in your damnable diaries.

(*UNCLE stands to walk away. They start to struggle again. Uncle is thrown back down onto the floor.*)

Stay down! I recall tabulated references from Kabbalistic literature; the *Zohar* and the *Chesed le-Abraham*, regarding these lost locations. Your mania even mentioned a city called Shamballa located close to the core.

UNCLE

No one asked you to read my jottings. I hid each volume for a purpose.

VERNE

The purpose being, according to ancient Dacian sagas, underground chambers occupied by an ancient goddess called Zalmoxis. In Mesopotamia, there is even the story of a man who, after traveling through the blackness of a tunnel in the mountain of Mashu, entered Her garden seeking immortality.

VOICE

(*Echoes.*)

They praised me. They praised me. As Deliverer and their Strength.

VERNE

Time and space are different there. Not as rational, or accommodating, as in our beloved Nantes. No Gallic morning, nor Loire-Atlantique noon, or seaport evenings. Instead, those terrible territories are characterised by the stark and endless heat of a blazing furnace.

(*He wipes his brow.*)

A perpetually active crematorium. A ceaseless pyre, wherein mastodons, teratorns, and wild megatheriums, roam.

UNCLE

I tried to protect your innocence.

VERNE

(*Lunges at UNCLE, straddles him then pins him down.*)

Sit still! My memory heard you talking of a chapel, bell tower, and penitential beds, on Station Island. The bell tower standing on a mound marking the original site of an entrance into purgatory. Was that my warning?

UNCLE

Enough.

(*Tries to throw VERNE off, but is pinned again with renewed force.*)

VERNE

Cold fusion. Have you heard of it, uncle? Those who went before us talked of nothing else when

I met with them on inversed continents. Fusion powering the inside: wherein lizard boys built their shadowy fortress. To them, we are livestock. They see themselves as our farmers. Having survived a cataclysm, which destroyed their world long, long, ago, they await a Uranian sign to return to our upper lands.

(*Beat.*)

I intend to author it, by describing the adventures of an expedition to the North Pole led by intrepid Captain Hatteras. In himself, Hatteras is convinced waters around the Pole aren't frozen. Perhaps this is why his crew mutiny? Nonetheless, my alter ego, with a few trusted men, continues his explorations. Thereby, a colleague, Doctor Clawbonny, constructs a snow house to winter the blizzards. And, once fortified in this stronghold, the swashbucklers fight for survival. Indeed, in my tale, these men make bullets from frozen mercury, while frightening polar bears away through remotely controlled explosions.

(*Beat.*)

Inevitably undeterred, Hatteras resumes his sacred quest. Striding across elemental islands to eventually climb an active volcano obscuring the Pole. He is a born combatant. His opponents being rampant fire and raging ice. Unsurprisingly, perhaps, he finds himself driven insane. I will additionally tell my readers that losing his "soul" in the chthonic caverns of the North has muted his mouth forever.

VOICE

(*Echoes.*)

My Summer Palace is the ever-burning Agartha. A flaming pyramid titled by some as the House of Fear. My Summer Palace. My ever-burning Agartha.

(*Beat.*)

(*Listening, the two of them struggle aggressively.*)

VERNE

(*Gaining the upper hand.*)

Alchemy, Teros, paranormal agitations, Deros, witches, and blazing imps. In my scientific romances, I will explain why such ideas are important. Undoubtedly, these fantastical cartographies of actual mathematical dimensions explore convex and concave facts: outlining the manner in which a ball may be turned inside out. Connecting our probable past with possible futures! Inside this topsy-turvy globe, I equally met Biblical giants who told me that the mark of Cain still scars their enormous foreheads. Can you give me an "amen" uncle? Can you? The sickness of Sin on parallel paths persists to taint our Earth. Admiral Byrd told me as much in a daydream. So did surviving members of the Nazi Party from the safety of New Berlin. Either way, each of these narratives comes to an untimely rest when considering those demons inside.

UNCLE

You are the slave of surface truths! Zalmoxis is the pattern of rebirth itself.

VERNE

There is a deep interior, and then there is the sunlight of flatlands. Safer places by half. Nonetheless, the beams of that inner sun are addictive; tending, as they do, towards black light. Maybe madness alone is the reward of intramural-lit journeying? Or the fruits of a much higher mind? At any rate, you will not live it.

(*VERNE starts to strangle uncle.*)

Entrances and exits, uncle. All the world's a transdimensional stage.

(*Beat.*)

(*Another ferocious struggle. Again, VERNE gets the upper hand.*)

VERNE

Because of your mystical semiotics, uncle, I discovered both Northern and Southern entrances to this supplementary sphere. Clearly, one opening is blocked by Ice. I also saw buried Lemuria, sunken Atlantis, and lost Pellucidar in my mind's eye. Beneath this, whilst traveling through altered states, I had lunch with Ludvig Holberg. By the way, he said you were one of the Megamicres, a race of multicoloured bisexual dwarfs, although, on reflection, they may be from *Icosaméron* by Giacomo Casanova. But, I digress. Taking seconds, I read Edgar Allan Poe's *The Narrative of Arthur Gordon Pym of Nantucket*, W. H. Hudson's *A Crystal Age*, Sir Edward Bulwer-Lytton's *The Coming Race*, and even *Plutonia* by Vladimir Obruchev. Indian summers and grilling tombs, uncle. All giving birth to new, sizzling, realities.

VOICE

(*Echoes.*)

Locations are made from primal substances due to the focus of innumerable minds. In time, they come to exist for everyone to visit. Such locations as Ba'dan, on the implied vectors of a calculated mirage.

(*Beat.*)

(*VERNE lets UNCLE go, reacting to the voice.*)

VERNE

Be this as it might, anyone shining brilliantly means they ignite more quickly. Similar to you and me uncle. In the hots of vision, we burn away. Besides, are we inside, or outside, uncle? Are we beneath, or on top? Oh, Midnight Sun, are you listening? Oh, Smokey god, forgive our weak perceptions. Take pity on us and Olaf Jansen, a Norwegian sailor, who claimed two years living amongst the inhabitants of your underground colonies. Critics eventually identifying the civilisation Jansen encountered with a submerged Tibetan castle of lore. Oh, incandescent gods, kindled beasts and fiery men. Oh yes, Nicholas Roerich included! Each one of these quixotic locations is roasting inside us.

UNCLE

But how much of it is true? All of it, none of it, or some of it?

(*He smiles at VERNE, straightens himself, and starts to read a book before exiting stage left.*)

VERNE

(*Turning to the audience as images of* A Journey to the Centre of the Earth, The Mysterious Island, Twenty Thousand leagues Under the Sea, *and* Around the World in Eighty Days *are projected onto the backdrop*).

Feasibly, one day I really will pen my own journey to the centre.

(Exit stage right.)

(Following a brief pause, UNCLE and VERNE return to take their bow and exit together stage left, whereas the DP remains on stage looking meditative.)

Lights down.

PRANK TWO:
A DAY IN THE LIGHT

Lights up.

(*DP dances the galliard in front of her audience. Behind her, the two ANGELS prepare for this second act.*)

DP

(*Addressing the audience.*)

This confrontation is set in Albert Schweitzer's Lambaréné hospital clinic in 1953. Late afternoon tea is being prepared by a local nurse named Nkwa, albeit the atmosphere in Albert's consulting room is tense. Inside the building Albert's loyal and devoted wife Helene waits for James Cameron's attack.

(*The two women enter stage left, while the men enter stage right.*)

JAMES

(*At the door.*)
Is he in?

NKWA

Afternoon tea is being served Mr. Cameron.

JAMES

Again, please call me James?

NKWA

Of course, Mr. Cameron. They are waiting for you. This way please.

JAMES

I know the way by now.

(*Testily, then singing.*)

"Picture you upon my knee. Just tea for two and two for tea."
(*Pushing the door open, JAMES walks up to ALBERT and firmly shakes his hand. He kisses HELENE lightly on the cheek and sits down opposite ALBERT at a small, occasional table. NKWA follows him inside.*)

ALBERT

Good afternoon James. Helene will be "mother" as you say in England and pour our refreshments.

JAMES

I am leaving in a few hours.

ALBERT

Yes, we know. May I be so bold as to ask what you intend to say about Helene and myself in the British press? We have both been wondering …

JAMES

Why wondering?

ALBERT

Because you have been so uncomfortable during the last few days. Everyone has noticed you have barely spoken a word.

JAMES

I suppose I feel like an upstart Julius Caesar visiting Egyptian Pharaoh. No matter where I look, the sun is too bright.

ALBERT

(*Jokingly.*)

A day in the sun god's light? That's nearly Biblical, James.

JAMES

Unlike Ptolemy XIII, you were a giant.

ALBERT

Were?

JAMES

You were a prominent music scholar and organist. Also, you grasped J. S. Bach's Chorale Preludes as rhythmic imagery. Illustrating themes from the Biblical texts these hymns were based on.

ALBERT

Serious music remains one of my inspirational passions.

JAMES

Much more significantly, your writings demonstrated how historical processes made Christ himself. The way in which innumerable models of this Saviour changed with period and purpose.

ALBERT

Actually, I was searching for the Holy.

JAMES

As I read! Explaining why you rejected most previous authors. Arguing Jesus must be understood in the light of His own convictions. Dependant, as these were, on Jewish eschatology in his era. A monumental act of deconstruction. Yet, you still found something Sacred beneath these literary veneers. A "reverence for life" in old dismantled dogmas. A revelation which won you the 1952 Nobel Peace Prize.

ALBERT

All past tenses.

JAMES

Not all.

(*Beat.*)

(*Helene moodily brings to the table a large silver tray with a teapot, china cups, and pastries. She begins to serve tea, although she is clearly upset.*)

HELENE

(*Intrusively.*)

It's akin to sedition! People nowadays seem incapable of achieving moral consciousness. We funded and practically built this hospital ourselves, James. It was an act of Christian charity.

JAMES

I remain fully aware of this Helene.

HELENE

Oh, are you James? Are you really? Albert even enrolled as an undergraduate physician, while simultaneously lecturing at Tübingen University in order to achieve his vision.

JAMES

Yes, he saw a second light.

HELENE

We left home on Good Friday in February 1913, hearing the voice of God Himself.

JAMES

A noble endeavour.

HELENE

(*Desperately.*)

Were we wrong?

JAMES

Times have changed Helene.

HELENE

I am being serious!

JAMES

So am I. To be honest Helene, Albert remains aloof from daily affairs like some latter-day Solar Hero shedding his rays of civilising light across poor old benighted Africa. It's an inappropriate stance to say the least.

HELENE

(*Pointedly.*)

Answer me! Should we feel guilty for healing the sick, defending hope, and bringing support to the downtrodden? In our day, duty spoke for itself. Albert and I weren't aiming to coerce anyone into cultural surrender. Our intentions were innocent.

JAMES

Nothing is innocent; and colonial Europe isn't a forgotten world.

HELENE

Its paternity endures.

ALBERT

(*Suddenly stands and contests.*)

We are creatures of reverence. Every organism in the Family-of-Life demands our service. Only then, in the midst of a shared and collective goodwill, shall peace become possible.

HELENE

(*Quickly following.*)

We accepted our burdens as creative freedoms.

ALBERT

(*Quickly following.*)

We claimed ethical choices as auguries of Soul.

HELENE

(*Quickly following.*)

The Gospels are about love; unconditional love.

JAMES

(*Contrarily.*)

So my grandfather told me.

ALBERT

Spirit speaks anew to each generation.

JAMES

For my generation, it communicates through impiety.

(*Beat.*)

HELENE

Your post-war world wants to pull down its previous idols. This is the real issue.

JAMES

Oh, let's break a few windows and breathe some fresh air! There are too few modern amenities here. Locals have scant training. The wards need cleaning. As our teachers used to write at the bottom of school reports in England, Albert "could do better."

HELENE

James, do you realise how hard it was for us in those early years? Whereas, nowadays, we are hardly in our prime. Albert is seventy-eight. Or, are we simply ageing Judas goats ready for sacrifice?

JAMES

I'm not your executioner.

(*Turning to NKWA with an extremely dirty look.*)

Okay, we tried it your way, but this isn't going to be fixed with herbs, chicken feathers, and some mumbled words.

NKWA

The Schweitzers brought genuine light into our lives. Otherwise, we'd want revenge, and that's what you want. Right enough, Mr. Cameron?

JAMES

(*Guiltily.*)

As much as you don't want to Nkwa, you hesitate before siding with them. The Schweitzers have made you in their autocratic image.

NKWA

Not really! Neither are we fools! Even before they arrived we understood that in the darkness things wither and die.

JAMES

(*Ignoring her.*)

Well, I suppose that's up to you. It's your revenge, after all.

NKWA

We want dignity Mr. Cameron, not revenge.

JAMES

As "junior brothers?"

NKWA

You find real humanitarianism blinding, Mr. Cameron.

The Schweitzers never claimed to be perfect.

JAMES

(*Angrily.*)

I don't like the way you are smiling at me nurse.

NKWA

(*Sarcastically.*)

Like an adult towards a petulant child? Our Elders say there are three hells in the darkness. I was wondering which one awaited you!

JAMES

And the son of the sun god will save everyone else? Hail Ra! Hooray, hurrah; Ra, Ra, Ra! He is a sun god, he is a fun god. He delivers all those who obey him.

HELENE

(*Anxiously.*)

This is truly outrageous! Our world wasn't wrong about everything. Back then, we experienced resistance to our work from all sides. Particularly from fellow Christians. To top it all, closed doors in Alsace-Lorraine were eventually accompanied by death threats when we arrived here.

NKWA

(*Standing her ground and staring at JAMES.*)

The first hell is malnutrition, both physical and spiritual. No tribe proceeds to industrial development without a leavening agricultural period. After all, we are all people of our time Mr. Cameron.

JAMES

Nothing has changed nurse!

NKWA

(*Continuing.*)

The second hell, they say, is populated by amputees. Those people who have lost parts of themselves. Whereas the third is a netherworld of enforced uniformity. Tribal medicine men speak little of this ultimate torment.

JAMES

And this third hell is for me?

NKWA

If you choose! Or, we can all ascend back into the Light, wherein things prosper and thrive. Upwards, and upwards, and upwards. Beyond mythology. Above fear. Impervious to words and phrases like "debunking" or "career move," whilst mindful of the overall good done by others.

JAMES

This conversation is leading nowhere. Goodbye to each of you. Maybe I will write an exposé, maybe I won't! Who knows? In any case, our final parting will be staged for the cameras – once my boat arrives.

(JAMES strides out of ALBERT's consulting room and exits stage left. The others quickly follow. For his part, ALBERT looks at JAMES and starts to speak in a saddened tone, but walks towards the audience.)

ALBERT

James, James, James, you are everybody

You are a loud voice on a wet London street

You are the frustrated life of a lazy lover

You are a weekend lost in cheap American beer

And the broken brown bottle of a barroom fight

You are an exaggeration of the Existential

You are the oppressor of lives

You are incarcerated

You are the peevish destroyer of worlds
You are the sulking need behind every last word
You are a lie!
Neither Arthur nor Mordred
The Son of Stars
Or purest slime
You are still the animal at each party
A half-eaten kebab on the way home
You are disloyal and jealous in equal measure
You are spineless
You are the subjunctive
Pleasuring yourself with yourself
You are the lone dancer on a nightclub floor
You are a credit card
You are also the night bus driving our neon Nirvana
Along filthy streets.
You are Postmodernity
You are empty
You are the unquestioning mind
You are the absence of Spirit
Because you have never amounted to anything.
Betraying your ancestors
Betraying your kith
Betraying your kinsfolk
Betraying the future,
You simply ignore death
And sickness, as the passing of an inconvenience.
Along with Great Nature

As an asset to be stripped.

(*Following a brief pause, everyone returns to take their bow. The angels clear away the drawings and exit stage left, while the DC prepares to stand in the dark thoughtfully.*)

Lights down.

PRANK THREE:
FATE'S GOOD FORTUNE

Directions.

Ideally, one side of the stage will have a gigantic Azerbaijani flag as its partial backdrop. Yet, the other side is completely darkened so the Sibyl's black expressionless, face is not fully visible. Obviously, as an archetypal figure, she is dressed from head to foot in white. In the meantime, a dead body is moved into position in order to lay in state on a raised platform in the centre. The angels enter stage left with this corpse.

Lights up.

DP

(*Facing the audience, but starting sketches.*)

These biographies differ from other scenarios by being taken from the point of view of a lone protagonist. A man of wealth and power who is driven by a single question of overarching importance to him as well as his emerging nation! In this regard, he meets the antithesis of his expectations in purgatory by encountering a black woman named Sibyl.

(*SIBYL enters stage right. She walks towards a chair near the head of the deceased President and sits. Of a sudden, the ghost of HEYDAR ALIYEV appears behind his own corpse and walks towards the audience in order to speak with them. Unlike his cadaver, ALIYEV's spirit is dressed in smart, but casual, clothes.*)

ALIYEV

I'm alive!

(*Looking at himself in a reassuring manner.*)

SIBYL

(*Clinically.*)

Of course you aren't. Otherwise, I would not be here with you.

ALIYEV

Then, I'm . . .

SIBYL

(*Clinically.*)

Taking your first steps into eternity.

(*Beat.*)

ALIYEV

(*Warmly.*)

Sibyl, my old friend, before I walk any further I need to know what kind of life I led from eternity's point of view. If I was a good man? What do you think? Was I a bad man? Had I achieved anything real? Did people love me? How many enemies have I made in my days? Perhaps, more importantly, did I do my duty?

(*Beat.*)

ALIYEV

Perhaps, having lost all points of reference, I can look again at the opportunities, and fated accident made by Her . . .

(*Points at SIBYL.*)

which framed my material moments; a passing phase, dare I say, although allowing the slow and majestic pulse of Azerbaijan to flow through my body. Yes, through the reflections of Being I can see those weeks at the beginning, as well as the end. I can watch as I stand here – the 13th March 1995 – when an armed insurrection aimed to bring me down. Look, look . . .

(*Gesticulating to the audience.*)

over there; a special unit of interior troops led by Colonel Rovshan Javadov. From this vantage point, I can also see four days later, on 17th March, when units of our Azerbaijani Armed Forces surrounded the insurgents in their camp to assault it. Yes, yes, yes, they are killing Javadov; a man who had forgotten the infirmity of our country before I returned to restore it to full vigour in those early months of real independence. A country with failing infrastructures, no oil revenue to speak of, and a population suffering from far too many privations. If I am honest, hardly anyone else would have agreed to take those poisoned reins of political power. But, it was my duty. Look, I can even view my birth on 10th May 1923 and my death in 2003.

(*Beat.*)

ALIYEV

(*Reflectively.*)

Who was I Sibyl? Merely the third President of Azerbaijan? Well, this much is certain I suppose. Gazing back between 1969 to 1982, I was the leader of Soviet Azerbaijan; more or less dominating political life. False ideas of duty were everything to me then. They were the crumbling capstone of my deflected purpose. Even when I married Zarifa in 1948! Look...

(*Pointing to the left.*)

it is happening in front of my eyes. On October 12th, 1955, during the birth of our daughter Sevil, these delusions obsessed me. Especially, when we had our son, my own Ilham in December 1961. I wanted a good future for him. For everyone! Ah, if I don't look away, I will be able to see Zarifa dying of cancer again, aaaah! I can feel my heart breaking.

(*Stares upwards in anguish.*)

Of course, Ilham became my pride and joy. I loved my daughter no less than him, but he was my heir. My future. My special gift to Azerbaijan. From where I am now, however, it all seems like yesterday; or maybe tomorrow.

SIBYL

I know these things Heydar. Is there anything else you want to tell me? Any hidden confession before moving on? Do you have any regrets?

ALIYEV

Who doesn't have regrets? We are not spirits like you. We are fleshy men and women. Living inside the pressures and pains of the physical world around us. I recall suffering a heart attack once, long ago. The pain was unbelievable, but nothing compared to the reassertion of Soviet control in Baku. Oh, that numbing, political, agony! After all, Black January witnessed the martyrdom of 137 innocent people; our own people; my kith, our kinsfolk. Adding another unnecessary tragedy to the bleak storms already brewing over Nagorno-Karabakh.

SIBYL

But you wore many faces when you were of Earth.

ALIYEV

We reincarnate every day. Minute by year. Second by season. At the start of each and every hour. You spirits construct us this way to satisfy your own ends. All of you worship evolution. The end result of things! Yet, humans are immediate. Look, there is innocent baby Heydar...

(*Points tangentially.*)

Then, there is Heydar the cocky schoolboy. A different Heydar lives there ...

(*Pointing downwards.*)

as a young man and student. Atop of this was a period when I held high rank in the Communist Party; rivalling Mikhail Gorbachev himself. Later...

(*Pointing to the right.*)

critics commented, I reinvented myself as a moderate nationalist. What did they know? Such men were deliberately blind to the continuous passion I felt for my culture, my friends, my family, and my country. For my beloved Azerbaijan! Its history. Its way of life. In us, East meets West. Maybe only in my home province of Nakhchivan, where I was an independent governor for a while, did they really see the man behind each of these expressions.

SIBYL

Were you ambitious? Most men confuse aspiration with ambition.

ALIYEV

Should a man have no aim in his life? Surly, what matters is good will? The force behind his drive. Clearly, during Elchibey's one year in power, I continued to govern Nakhchivan without subordination to the official government in Baku. Unlike him, I believed in keeping public freedom as a facet of duty. This much is true! Proved, furthermore, when the Popular Front's Minister of the Interior, Isgandar Hamidov, attempted to forcibly overthrow me. But, by this time, the people knew me! So, unsurprisingly, he found himself thwarted by local militia at the regional airport. Indeed, they spontaneously arose in my defence. For love of my people, I even negotiated a cease-fire agreement in

Nakhchivan with the then President of Armenia, Levon Ter-Petrosyan. Critics tend to forget this.

(*He looks at SIBYL.*)

Nevertheless, in this place without context, events replay themselves forever. I can watch once more 9th June 1993 when, following a military coup in Ganja led by Colonel Surat Huseynov, my would-be rival Abulfaz Elchibey was forced to invite me to Baku in order to mediate this crisis. All culminating, on 24th June – amidst the advancement of insurgent forces under Huseynov's control – in Elchibey fleeing the city to return to his native village of Keleki. The conclusion was obvious. By August 1993, Elchibey was stripped of his presidency in a nationwide referendum. October 1993 saw me elected President. What was it Shakespeare said, "Some have greatness thrust upon them?" To my own understanding, I knew what he meant. Occasionally, a man's freedom is found only through performing his duties.

SIBYL

What about your failures and secret conceits? Few realise the way someone surmounts an obstacle shows his, or her, true character.

ALIYEV

Time makes us Sibyl. It breaks each one of us too. I tried, but failed, to resolve the Nagorno-Karabakh conflict, which, by summer's end 1993, had resulted in the loss of 16 percent of Azerbaijan's rightful territory, as well as 30,000 deaths. Nowadays, roaming refugees and displaced itinerants mark this beautiful region like a scar. As surgeons, we attempted a counter-offensive in December, but failed to regain control of Kalbajar, Fuzuli, or Khojavend, ending up with heavy losses. Every one of them injuring me personally: making me an additional casualty. By May 1994, Azerbaijan entered into a fitful ceasefire, which continues to tempestuously hold. Nonetheless, this issue is an open wound for Azerbaijan, because Armenia still occupies our Nagorno-Karabakh.

SIBYL

Was it all worth it? Since you are now beyond favour, blame, and grace. What type of footprint did you make on your world above becoming a statue in a town square?

ALIYEV

I did my duty! Admittedly, I was not perfect. How could I be? Can a man be made imperfect and then judged by the standards of perfection? On one hand, both I and my people may trace our proud ancestors through the trading cities of the Silk Road into antiquity. On the other hand, we are newborn. Modern Azerbaijan itself merely twenty, or so, years old. Western powers may posture, along with darker influences from the East; wanting to judge us by standards it has taken them centuries to achieve. But, we are a fresh idea. We will take the best from past experience and embrace futurity. We will show the nations around us how great human beings can become.

SIBYL

I hardly spoke to the Emperor Claudius when he asked me similar questions to yours. Except, that is, from mentioning his body had housed a one-time ruler of the Roman Empire. Sometimes, however, it is Fate's good fortune to meet with men like you. Rare men Heydar, that others detect to be distinct, while finding themselves incapable of placing their finger on the difference. Men who love to fight for something better. Whose self-sacrifice makes the world a brighter place! When boys, you Azerbaijanis admired the fastest runner and the toughest wrestler. Truly, Azerbaijanis love a winner and will not tolerate a loser. Above this, you understand teams. And a nation, if it is to survive, is a team. It lives, eats, sleeps, and struggles as a team. Equally, Azerbaijanis know all real heroes are neither lone warriors, nor solitary storybook fighters. They are the men who step up to history's measure mindful of others. Those who shoulder the responsibility of building a collective dream. The type of vision which remoulds their world into a warmer, lighter, and happier sphere. You, Heydar, were such a dutiful man.

(*ALIYEV turns to THE SIBYL, raises his arms in adoration, takes a step forward and disappears. Following a brief pause, the two players take a bow together and leave by either side of the stage.*

Thereafter, the ANGELS stand either side of the DP before themselves leaving stage left.)

Lights down.

EPILOGUE

Stage directions.

The song I Lost My Heart to a Starship Trooper *starts to play before lights up. Thereupon, the two silver ANGELS return as two moths who rush around before initiating a Busby Berkeley synchronised tap routine. Following a few verses of this song, a giant green skull descends behind everyone. It then opens into two parts in order to allow a manly manifestation of the DP to emerge. Immediately, he interlaces his arm with his female counterpart like the Eternal Champion of Humanity. The Divine Rebis itself! Anyway, this other DP is dressed as a clinician. So, the DP's womanly half takes her position on a couch at the same time as the physician sits in a chair at the front of the stage.*

DP WOMAN

I performed in Pompeii Pompeii and acted alongside the trans actress Shrinking Violet and her lesbian lover Foghorn. Of course, trans women are full women, period. What is more, I also enjoyed coffee with Cavafy until we set off to Flic-en-Flac in the summertime. Accompanied, as we were, by a small moth outside a camper and a big moth with a hairspray.

DP MAN

Do you hate this time of year? You once said it was peopled by idiots and insects. And mad sunbeams and cotton clothes. You said it was not an old moth time, or a dressing-up time. Instead, it might be playtime for a small moth and his moth-friend. A big moth with his hairspray and a small moth by a camper.

BIG MOTH

We Moths were living in their clothes there,
Because, we enjoyed eating all the clothes there,
With salt and pepper and serving spoons
And wet wipes and a paper towel
Since, we were hungry, but fashionistas, too.

DP MAN

Look Pilot. Look Pilot. Dear Miss Pilot,
Rather than sleeping under trees by the Seaside,
Let's get lippy and conditioner and other makeup too.
Let's go and have fun with the moths in the camper with the clothes there. Using prongs and the tongs and all the curlers too and parade in the shade of the

camper by the seaside.

SMALL MOTH

I'll dress like a Chef with those clothes in our cupboard

Before getting wigs and wands and aprons and apricots

Then, let the dogs with clogs come, or the bats with hats come

Let the dogs and bats with clogs and hats come

To our camper with its pink fashion passion

Like a Clown, or a King, or a cocktail, or a clock.

So, come to knit and stitch and sew

With needles that weave and weft and warp and hitch

For a Moth with a hairspray and a Moth in the camper,

Along a ruffle on the road for fans of perky Turkey.

BIG MOTH

But, not China by the diner

Where Aladdin pulled his punches on a carpet in the sky

And Imams placed a genie in a lamp for safekeeping.

(*The entire cast gathers behind the couch of the original DP in dimmed light suggesting they are her thoughts and dreams.*)

ALL

But, unlike Aladdin, what about women when seen as property?

(*Beat.*)

If women choose, after all, not out of fear, but out of joy, to speak their testimonies, then there is something magical in their words.

(*Beat.*)

Lesbians, sex workers, wives, trans, spinsters, mothers, nuns, singers, medics, teachers, lawyers, suffragettes, Eve, dancers, priests, astronauts, soldiers, mathematicians, Our Blessed Theotokos, each telling a story never spoken before. Each narrating a unique truth no one else can say in the way they would tell it.

(*Beat.*)

We are no longer women in Mayhem, but the voice of Liberation.

(*Everyone bows as the original DP stands and stretches her arms in the air through vindication. The house lights are blinding at that moment. Thereafter, the moths ask members of the audience for their judgement about the characters onstage.*)

Lights down.

NOTES

The original production of *A Day in the Light* premiered on December 11, 2014, at 6:30 p.m. at the House of Lords, Committee Room 4a thank to the invitation of Professor the Lord Laird of Artigarvan and Dr. Roger Prentis. The cast was:

ALBERT SCHWEITZER Peter Revel-Walsh
MADAME HELENE SCHWEITZER Delianne Forget
JAMES CAMERON Valentin Hripko
NURSE NKWA Priscilla Fere

Writer, Director, and Producer David William Parry
Director's Assistant Inessa Amber
Technical Support Alex Metslov

Fate's Good Fortune, a single act tragicomedy for voices originally uploaded to YouTube on February 17, 2015, in a London, UK, private studio. The cast was:

PRESIDENT HEYDAR ALIYEV Peter Revel-Walsh
THE SIBYL Priscilla Fere

Writer, Director, and Producer David William Parry
Recorded and Designed Paul Obertelli

AN AFTERWORD BY REINHARD AUER

David William Parry is a stupendous man. All of England knows him as a religious leader and an author. He graduated in religious studies and composed his doctoral thesis on the French Christian existential philosopher Gabriel Marcel. Indeed, Parry has also served as a preacher, Bible teacher, and senior pastor while being involved actively in the LGBTQIA+ movement. All at the same time as authoring numerous books and essays. As such, he is extremely well-educated with a great knowledge of God, the Bible, and the occult.

He has additionally been connected with theatre for a long time and has recently been recognised as a playwright. Everything meaning, his second play *Women in Mayhem* is due to premiere in the Camden Fringe 2024. Overall, Parry himself calls the play a "nonsense dramedy," which is why it seems to be a dramatic bastard. After all, the play consists of three acts (called "pranks") with a prologue and epilogue causing each scenario to oscillate between serious drama and comical sketch sequences. Yet, it is about women who are trans, heterosexual, and lesbian, who find themselves in various worlds.

But they appear, in a way, to cause critics to wonder whether they are actually the same people "acting in different environments" despite their ethnic differences, despite their class affiliation. Or maybe these various characters are just aspects of a single psyche? Certainly, in the epilogue audiences themselves need to decide whether these character concepts are as they are presented to be …

So, Rev. Parry presents us with a tricky situation. His chaos is reminiscent of Purgatory, with a guide, a figure, called the "Dancing Pilot," like Dante's Virgil. The content of the piece therefore has all the hallmarks of Absurd Theatre, or a series of pictures by Dali, although centering around theatrical pivots (a black box, the Hospital of Albert Schweitzer, a mortuary in Azerbaijan). Now, even formally, the author has big shoes to fill. In which case, Parry is asking that you believe yourself to be in a scenario by Artaud, in which women ultimately emerge as polyvalent beings, whilst leading audiences to suspect, "We are no longer women in Mayhem, but the voice of Liberation." Well, this "plot" is extremely sophisticated – on the one hand nonsense, on the other very enlightening. It looks like a well-made three-act play, even though it juggles with the constant change of reality and imagination. Provoking questions along the lines that maybe these characters are not people at all but dreams and illusions. Or, is this an inventory of roles in a psycho- or socio-drama à la Jacob Moreno? In any case, the piece can claim a certain originality, particularly due to the fact audiences can give it a critical relevance by agreeing or disagreeing with its conclusions. Is it revolutionary (as the author thinks)? Perhaps a question only the angels accompanying the main character (who appear as moths in the epilogue) can answer alongside invited members of the audience.

Vienna
March, 2024

BIOGRAPHY

Reinhard Auer was born in 1948 in Linz, Upper Austria. He pursued his studies in Philosophy and History at the University of Graz, Sociology and Economics at the Johannes Kepler University Linz, and Theatre Sciences and Directing at the University of Vienna. From 1976-80, he attended the Masterclass of Directing at the Institute of Theatre Sciences Vienna, under the tutelage of Professor Wolfgang Glueck. Auer served as the assistant director of Satel Film and ORF (Austrian Broadcast and Television) from 1979-80.

In 1980, Reinhard Auer founded the Theatre of Spittelberg and Yura-Soyfer-Theatre of Vienna and served as its Director until 1992. Since 1993, he has been the Artistic Director of the Liberty Theatre of Bolzano in Italy. He is also a member of the International Theatre Institute ITI (Austrian delegate) since 2002 and has served as the CEO of some Artists' Associations in Austria and Italy.

Reinhard Auer has received several awards and honours throughout his career. He was awarded the Cross of Honour for Science and Art of the Republic of Austria and the Golden Medal of Merit of the City of Vienna. He has directed over 130 theatre productions in 19 countries and has received three international awards for directing

(Ukraine, Czech Republic, Serbia) and many international awards for productions in countries like Russia, Cyprus, Georgia, Armenia, China, Romania, etc.

www.ingramcontent.com/pod-product-compliance
Lightning Source LLC
Chambersburg PA
CBHW031426040426
42444CB00006B/707